Dedication

This is dedicated to the families and
individuals   who have lived in Rock Island (Ft. Worth,
Texas), 4th and 5th Ward (Houston, Texas), and
the neighborhoods of San Antonio, Texas.

I also would like to dedicate this manuscript to My Love -
Christina, my family and friends. But most of all, I would
like to dedicate this to my Lord and Savior- Jesus Christ,
thank you for including me into your service.

Table of Contents

Forward

The modern church has abandoned the inner city for the sociologists to dissect and interpret, the Boys and Girls Clubs to serve, and the police and the courts to control. The result is a spiritual vacuum that few seem to care about. The former downtown and inner city churches have fled to the suburbs where they have a parish of respectable, fairly affluent, middle-class people with whom to work. The emphasis in today's church is upon survival and growth, members and money, safety and security rather than obedience to Christ's obvious concern for the poor, the prisoner and the oppressed.

In His inaugural sermon, Jesus quoted Isaiah the prophet in proclaiming, "The Spirit of the Lord is upon me, because he has anointed me to preach good news to the poor. He has sent me to proclaim freedom for the prisoners, and recovery of sight for the blind, to release the oppressed, to proclaim the year of the Lord's favor" (Luke 4:19-19). Here and there one finds a few courageous men and women who heed the words of Jesus and determine to invest their lives in those who make up the under-class of our nation, the poor and oppressed who are abundantly present in every city in the United States. Brian Bockmon is one of these courageous disciples of Jesus who has a heart for the inner city.

The author writes, not out of ivory tower research, but from the rich treasure of personal involvement and experience with his subject material. From his college years onward, he has invested his life in ministering to young people in the inner city. He understands the dynamics of gang life, the absence of parental guidance, the cycle of poverty, the danger of violence, and the heart cry for love and acceptance which are the sum of these young people's life experiences.

The theme of this book is the author's burden for the church to fulfill its purpose and minister to all people, regardless of race or socio-economic standing. It is practical and realistic. Perhaps the author's greatest contribution is his emphasis upon the absolute necessity of establishing long-term, loving relationships with inner city youth if they are to be reached for Christ. The words of the chorus, "They will know we are Christians by our love, by our love..." is never more appropriate than in this setting.

The book is easy to read, but difficult to assimilate into one's conscious behavior. There is no more difficult place to serve than the inner city, but there is also no field so white unto harvest. Brian Bockman awakens our sleeping consciences and alerts us to the call of Christ to "go into all the world and make disciples." He reminds us that we need not go to a third world country to minister "to the least of these." That world is only a few miles away, a world we drive past on our daily commutes, a world that seemingly only Christ cares about.

The title of the book says it all—*IF THEY'RE GOOD ENOUGH FOR JESUS...THEY BETTER BE GOOD ENOUGH FOR ME.* It is a clarion call for the church to be the church in the here and now of the inner city. The modern church dare not neglect the poor, the prisoner, and the oppressed. To do so is to ignore the example of the Son of God whom we as Christian disciples are commanded to emulate.

Dr. Dick Maples
Retired Pastor

Chapter One: The Problem

THE PSALM OF THE GANGSTER

The gang is my shepherd
I shall always think I'm bad.
It makes me lay my life in danger,
And hold my colors high.
It leads me to juvenile detention,
County Jail, and Prison.
It destroys me and my family.
It leads me to the cemetery to say
Good-bye to my homeboy.
As I hold on to my pride I walk through the
Valley of memories of all the homeboys
That are dead, or locked up,
Because of gang violence.
My gang tries to comfort me, but how can they?
I've seen gang violence kill my homies
In the presence of their fathers and mothers,
Their wives, and their children.
My mind runneth over all the drive-by killings, Constantly
thinking of when my time will come. Surely, revenge and
death shall follow me
All the days of my life,
And I shall live in the
House of the Damned forever.

-Unknown

To begin this book, I would like you to ask yourself a simple question. If Jesus were here today, in a physical body, where would He be? Would He be in a suburban mega church? Would He be in your church? Or would He be ministering to the needy of the inner city? Please take a moment to ask the Lord to open your eyes to what He might be saying to you.

Now back to the question at hand. To find the answer to this, I think we should go to the Bible to see where Jesus' heart was and is. In the ninth chapter of Matthew, it says that Jesus was going through towns and villages, preaching the good news and healing the sick. It also says that when He saw the crowds, He had compassion on them because they were harassed and helpless, like sheep without a shepherd. Now doesn't this sound like America today? Throughout the gospels, Jesus associated Himself with the leprous, prostitutes, tax collectors, the poor, the down and out, the filthy and stinky, and the vulgar. Jesus ministered to the "sinners" of the world. This was radical. It doesn't seem that the clergy of that day liked to associate with ALL people. Are we any different? Ouch! Now, where would Jesus be today?

One might ask, "Why are the inner city neighborhoods the way they are?" Well, in the late sixties and throughout the seventies, an exodus took place. A man named Martin Luther King emerged and led an historic struggle that brought about an era of reconciliation among the races. Public schools were opened to ALL children and fair economic housing legislation was enacted. Opportunities started to open up for families who lived downtown. Store merchants gradually started to move their businesses out to areas of greater financial gain. Professional and trade people found new and more profitable areas of occupation. People who could now afford better homes moved to better neighborhoods. It seemed that stable families moved out while fragmented families stayed. Homes gave way to deteriorated rentals. Crime rate moved up and more families moved out. The traditional family was replaced by the gangs.[1] The downfall was like a domino effect and left a great void which was filled with darkness. The light slowly dimmed.

Lt. Mark Krey, of the Fort Worth, Texas Police Department agrees that gangs are becoming a replacement for the family. He states that as the demographics of an established urban neighborhood change, whether by an increase in minorities or a decrease in social economics, the inhabitance also begins to change. This causes an increase in violent activities such as burglary, rape, and even murder. The neighborhood becomes a self-perpetuating problem as it continues to decline.[2] Consider a Fort Worth case study during the exodus when people started to move to the surrounding suburbs and crime rose. Between 1970 and 1980, crime in Fort Worth, Texas, went up 73.1% and between 1980 and 1990, crime went up another 66.2%[3]

Now someone might point out that the Bible says that things are going to get worse until Jesus comes back and there is nothing we can do about it. It has been said, "Why polish brass on a sinking ship?" Why do people jog, even though

---

[1] Robert D. Lupton, Ph. D, Return Flight (Atlanta: FCS Urban Ministries, 1993). P. 15-19.

[2] Interview with Lt. Mark Krey, Fort Worth Police Department, Fort Worth, Texas, August 22, 1996.

[3] Research Department, Fort Worth Police Department. Uniform Crime Report 1970-1995.

they know they are going to die? Never let the second coming of Christ keep you from making an impact in our world.[4]

The problem we have in the inner cities is not sinners. Sinners sin. They don't have the Source (Jesus Christ) to resist temptation. They are a slave to sin.[5] Christians are called to be salt and light in this world.[6] Are we being salt and light in our community, in the work place, and even downtown? Are we loving the unlovable and sharing the most important thing in our lives with them? I guess you could say it is our fault that things are the way they are.[7]

One might wonder what it means to be "salt" and "light." This writer believes that the people who heard these words of Jesus knew what He meant. Back then, salt was used widely to preserve and to enhance the taste of food. As Christians, we should allow Christ to move in our lives in such a way where He keeps life fresh and full of zest. Let's not forget that there is another characteristic of salt. If salt gets into a cut or sore, it burns! We need to call sin for what it is and live lives of no compromise. As far as light is concerned, in a pitch dark room when a flashlight is turned on, one can see where he's going. The world does not know where it is going and people are wandering in darkness. We should let Christ shine in us so that EVERYBODY can glorify God and respond to His saving grace.[8]

What is sad is that some Christians don't realize this. Now let me give you two true stories. The names have been

---

[4] Dr. Tony Evans, Chapel Sermon, East Texas Baptist University, Spring 1992.
[5] John 8:34
[6] Matthew 5:13-16
[7] Dr. Tony Evans, Chapel Sermon, East Texas Baptist University, Spring 1992.

[8] Matthew 5:13-16

changes to protect the innocent. There's a church that got excited about all the inner city kids who accepted Christ one summer in their summer program and saw it as a means of bolstering their Sunday school enrollment. It was a great idea to reach out to the children, but the Sunday school teachers were not prepared to deal with non-churched kids. Many of the teachers threatened to quit after a couple of weeks if these kids continued to come. So the bus ministry fell to the wayside. The second situation involves a friend of mine who is a youth minister. When he first arrived to the church, they were averaging about three youth in Sunday school and about five youth on Wednesday night. Within several months, 30 to 35 youth were attending Sunday school and 40 to 50 youth came in on Wednesday nights. Christ was impacting the lives of this community in a **BIG WAY!** Teens were accepting Christ as their Lord and Savior and recommitting their lives left and right. Sounds exciting, right? Well, there were members in the church who weren't too excited and tried to cause problems. You see, he wasn't bringing the *"right"* type of kids. **Yuck!** They wanted him to bring in teens from "good Christian homes." The Lord brought in those who were hurting and in need of a Savior and someone who actually cared for them. As a result of the lack of support and the continuous pressure on forcing out these youth, the youth minister and ministry was gone in two years.

As the body of Christ, who is called to go into all the nations to proclaim the Gospel of Jesus Christ, we need to put down our prejudices and our wants and see the world as Christ sees it and follow after Him. To chase after Him with **EVERYTHING** you got!!! This book is not a step-by-step program to minister to inner city young people, but an attempt to allow the Lord to open your eyes to encourage you to work in His harvest field.

Chapter Two: The Culture

THA' SOME GAME

We have a game we all play.
Some get hurt and some will pay.
Some are losers and some are winners.
Some are frowners and some are downers.
But it is this cruel world we will play,
For we know what will happen the next day.
Lovers' lies get in the way,
But we live in this world of dismay.
So if next time someone asks you to play…
Just walk away.
'Cause each day wasn't worth to stay.

Billy Joe Perales

When the Lord started taking me to the inner city, I realized that the people were different from myself. They weren't raised in the same environment that I was raised in. Their values and their thought patterns were different from my own. Even though I wasn't in a different country, I was still embracing a different culture.

The English word, "culture," is used several different ways. There is even considerable debate among anthropologists (people who study customs, development, races, etc. of man) on how the term *culture* should be defined. For our purposes, we will define culture as "the more of less integrated ideas, feelings, and values and their associated patterns of behavior and products shared by a group of people who organize and regulate what they thing, feel, or do."[9]

Now if one looks back at this definition, one would notice that it has three dimensions to it: ideas, feelings, and values. The first dimension is a cognitive one. This aspect of culture has to do with the knowledge shared by members of a group or society. To go a step deeper into the culture, one embraces the affective dimension. This dimension has to do with the feelings people have – with their attitudes, ideas of beauty, likes and dislikes, tastes in food and dress, and ways if enjoying themselves or experiencing sorrow. For example, people in some cultures like their foods hot and spicy while others like their food cold. Now the evaluative dimension deals with the values of a culture in which it judges human relationships to be moral or immoral and what is right and wrong. It also deals with whom they put their faith and trust in.[10]

When one enters a new culture or sub-culture, a sense of excitement and fear comes upon them. As human beings, we get excited about new adventures in life, but we don't accept change very well. Culture shock happens to everybody. The difference is how one handles the situation. When one is going through culture shock, it is nice to know that it is a normal human reaction to change. At first, the culture is interesting and full of fascination. We are outside the new culture looking in. After a while, we move from being outside visitors to becoming cultural insiders. No longer is this strange culture exciting. Now it seems mysterious and impossible to learn. Here is where one gets frustrated and

---

[9] Paul G. Hiebert, <u>Anthropological Insights for Missionairies</u> (Grand Rapids, Michigan: Baker Book House, 1985). P. 30.
[10] Ibid. p.30-33

must decide to stay and adjust or move on. If one does not handle it right, they'll tend to hang on to their "home" culture like a two-year-old fighting to keep a toy. *Mine! Mine!* Eventually, everything is done in their "home" culture is the way it is supposed to be. Now, when one begins to laugh at himself and the situation, it is a good sign that recovery is beginning. And when one feels comfortable in their new culture and has learned enough to function efficiently without feelings of anxiety, then there is recovery from culture shock.[11]

Can you imagine the culture shock Jesus went through? Being in very nature God, on the throne in heaven, the majesty, the glory, and honor and all that came with it was left behind. It was all left behind so he could enter a "culture" where in the beginning, He was totally helpless. As a baby, He couldn't even defend Himself. He needed someone else to care for Him, feed Him, clothe Him, and change Him. And then on the cross, He experienced our sin. The One who had no sin took our sin upon Himself. This brings a deeper understanding of Romans 5:8, "But God demonstrates His own love for us in this: While we were still sinners, Christ died for us."[12] It amazes me time after time just how much the God of all gods, the King of all kings, the Creator of all that there is could love us so much.

Many of the people who live in the inner city areas and multi-housing areas look at the church in a three-part package: the church is only interested in their money, putting a notch on their Bible, and building numbers. Some believe that the world owes them, while others are doing whatever they can to survive. At the same time, let's not stereotype

---

[11] Ibid. p. 74-76.
[12] The Bible, (New International Version).

them. Each "hood" or neighborhood is constructed differently in its culture. They have their own rules, codes, and customs which one does not cross. It reminds me of I Corinthians 9:22-23, where Paul says, "To the weak I became weak, to win the weak. I have become all things to all men so that by all means I might save some." We need to drop pride in our own culture and embrace the culture and try to relate. The more you embrace, the further you'll understand the culture.

All throughout history, "Christians" have gone in the name of Christ to force "heathens" into salvation. Just look at the "holy wars". The "Christian" English were going to war to take back Jerusalem from the Muslims and convert them to Christianity. That's right...WAR! Is that crazy or what?

Back in the early 1960s, Don Richardson was a missionary to the Sawi people of Netherlands New Guinea. The Sawi people were headhunters and cannibals who saw treachery as a way of life. It was the ideal. To set up your victim for the kill, to gain the victim's trust was the ultimate! For to them, "to fatten with friendship" was the highest form of treachery. When the Gospel was presented to them, they looked upon Judas as the hero! His betrayal kiss was regarded as the ultimate expression of treachery. How can Christ impact *their* lives? Well...He did in a big way and he used Don and his wife to reach them.[13] They embraced the culture and waited for the Lord to show them the "key" to sharing the Good News to the Sawi people. We need to be willing to learn to try understanding the new culture and follow the Lord of the Harvest as He opens doors to go through.

Yes, I know that the inner city areas are here in the United States. Yes, they are not located in a foreign country. One can

---

[13] Don Richardson, Peace Child (Ventura, CA: Regal Books, 1974)

find the world in the inner cities. Just about every Central and South American country is represented on the east side of Houston, Texas. I remember growing up and watching *School House Rock* on Saturday mornings. One of the *School House Rock* episodes was about how America is like the great melting pot. A drive downtown in some of the metropolitan areas will prove this to be true. In the first chapter of Acts, Christ says that we are going to be His witnesses throughout the world.[14] Doesn't that include every nook and cranny of the world? I believe it does.

As you can tell, this is not an overnight deal. It's not like pulling out a "*4 Spiritual Laws*" tract and then going on your way. It takes an investment of your time and life, but the rewards are **FANTASTIC!** Are you willing to be on the cutting edge for Christ? Are you willing to invest your life in those that most people would ignore? Please take a moment to ask the Lord to open your heart to what He might be saying. I don't want you to think that the inner city is the only place to serve, but we need to be willing to let the Lord use us wherever and however He leads us.

---

[14] Acts 1:8

Chapter Three: Lordship

A POEM DEDICATED TO MY HOMEBOY

As I lay here by the stream,
I fall asleep into a dream.
I see myself crying before a grave,
'Cause my homeboy has gone away.
Six feet deep,
Is where my homie sleeps.
I pray to the Lord,
For his soul to keep.
For a tear of sadness
Escapes my eye,
'Cause I felt so bad inside.
For I won't see my homie no more,
But I know he has gone with the Lord.

Billy Joe Perales

The priority for a Christian in ministry or for life in general should be **CHRIST!** When one accepts Christ into their life, they're not only getting "fire insurance", but also they are pledging their allegiance and lives to follow Jesus Christ. In other words, **Christ is Boss!**

Too often, one hears about abusive employers who treat their employees with contempt causing fear. After graduating from college, I took my degree and started to do food preparation in a Buffalo Wing restaurant. No, buffaloes do not have wings. While I was there, life was rough. The owner

If They're Good Enough for Jesus . . .

was a former pro-football player who still had the same mentality. The stress of not making a mistake was high. It is not that way with our Lord Jesus Christ. He loves us so much that He gave His life for us. He is there for us, taking our burdens upon Himself. I'm not saying that we won't go through hard times – just the contrary. Satan is like a roaring lion and he will do anything to destroy our witness.[15] It is great that our heavenly Father is there to comfort us and carry us through those hard times. I'm sure if you would look back in your life, you can see the times where the Lord has brought you through troubled waters. **Isn't God GREAT?**

I heard a pastor preach about authority once and he said something which stayed with me to this day. He said that too many times we pray, "Help me" prayers. That is, "Lord, help me be a better Christian…" or "Lord, help me resist temptation…" We don't give Jesus full authority in our lives…we just need His help to get us over the hump. If He is Lord, then He is LORD! Lord of all means **TOTAL CONTROL.**

It seems that sometimes ministries survive on "programology." Planning programs first, *then* praying that the Lord would bless their plans. Isn't that like placing the cart before the horse? When I was in school at East Texas Baptist University, I was challenged by Troy, who would not prepare a sermon *until* the Lord had shown him what to say. We do have a part, a big part in ministry, but whose strength do we go in? Shouldn't it be in His strength?

In the wilderness, Moses and the children of Israel followed the direction of the Lord. Moses said to God, "If Your Presence does not go with us, do not send us from

---

[15] 1 Peter 5:8.

14

here."[16] In other words, Moses didn't want to take a step without God. We need to seek His vision, His guidance, and in His power!

Where there is no vision, people perish. [17] Just like it was said before about "programology," we need to seek where He's moving and join in with Him. As I said before, too many people try to move ahead of Him. Sometimes, do you think that just maybe the Lord might be saying, "Wait, and let me show you what I can do." God is alive and well and we need to adjust our lives to what He is about to do. If we are not seeking Him in a relationship, then how are we supposed to know what He's doing?

A thought went through my mind a couple of days ago. "What's the difference between vision and guidance?" When one thinks about it, they are very similar in nature, but vision and guidance are not exactly alike. The *Scribner-Bantam English Dictionary* says that vision is the act of seeing and guidance is direction or supervision.[18] When one talks about vision in the Christian life, one is usually referring to seeing the world and life as Christ views it. Now, guidance is looked at in several different ways. Some use a "fleece" mode, where they want to make sure, make sure, make sure that God is in something before they'll take a step. Personally, I prefer the "faith" method. That is, if the Lord opens a door, then step through it. If He opens another one, then step through it next. Keep going till the Lord shuts the door. He usually opens a window to climb through when He shuts a door. We just need

---

[16] Exodus 33:15.
[17] Proverbs 29:18.
[18] Edwin B. Williams, The Scribner-Bantam English Dictionary. (Toronto: Bantam Books; 1985) p. 405, 1014.

to be patient and trust in Him even more when that door shuts.

When I was in college, I was applying for my third term as a summer missionary in four summers. It all started out with my picking up the application and filling it out. Then, I turned it in and signed up for an interview with the Texas A & M University Baptist Student Union Missions ministry team. After that, the Lord opened the door to move on to apply for the state B.S.U. missions. After that, the Lord opened a door to go to Dallas for an interview. This was the last step before being appointed as a State B.S.U. missionary. Two days before I was to drive to Dallas, I received a call from my mentor in the ministry whom I had served under as a summer missionary in the mission program along the border in Brownsville, which is the most southern tip of Texas. My heart leaped with joy when he asked me to be his assistant, but I didn't know what to do. I had to tell Dwight of my interview, and that I would pray about it. I prayed and gave it over to the Lord for His complete control. I was denied the appointment, but I knew at the same time that the Lord was shutting one door and opening another for me to be Dwight's assistant. It was a **great** summer in which I was able to see the Lord *bring in the harvest!* People were praying to accept Christ left and right. **WHOOP** (A Texas Aggie expression of exhilaration.)! It was also a privilege to work with Dwight the following three summers, too. The Lord taught me so much about missions and ministry through Dwight. It was simply taking a step of faith through the doors the Lord was opening and trusting Him to shut the doors to direct me.

There is only so much that we can do in our own strength. Too many times we trust in our own strength and abilities. There is a higher power source in which people tend not to use...and that is Jesus Christ. It seems that here in America people trust in their own abilities, their own talents, and their own strengths more than anything else - a "pull yourself by your own bootstraps" mentality. Yes, we need to be able to stand up on our own, but at the same time to be in total dependence upon Christ.

I remember the first summer that I was Dwight's assistant; I got to see the Lord do some incredible things. In the ministry down there, youth groups would come down for a week at a time on mission trips. About twenty-seven groups come down in about a nine-week period to do Vacation Bible Schools on both sides of the border. We had two 30 foot by 60 foot circus tents that we would put up if a group was at a site with too little shade. As a result of vandalism, we had to set up the tents daily. One week that summer, we had a safe site to leave one of the tents up all week. One night early in the week, a storm came off the coast. When we arrived the next morning, we were told that the tent had collapsed and had a 6 foot tear in it. Immediately, the tent crew and I hurried in the rain to salvage the tent. When we arrived, we noticed that one of the two aluminum poles had blown down while the other had just sunk about a foot in the mud. We loaded the boards, poles, chains, and stakes in the back of my truck. Then we had to fold up the tent in the rain. That means that we had a lot of extra weight because of the added water. The four of us struggled over and over again to lift the tent off the ground. Between the extra weight and the slipping in the mud, we just could not do it. Then Ian had an idea, "Let's pray!" What a concept! We prayed for strength and glorified His name. After the prayer, the tent came right up. We carried the tent to my truck and loaded it. **Praise God!** It was like we had an angel on each end of the tent.

It wasn't us one bit. Our weakness was made perfect by His strength. It was not because we were "super spiritual" or anything like that. It was **all** Jesus. We just trusted in Him and He came through in flying colors. It reminds me of the popular verse in Proverbs, "Trust in the Lord with all your heart and lean not on your own understanding. In all ways acknowledge Him and He will direct your path."[19] In the letter to the Philippians, Paul writes that it is Christ that gives him strength.[20] Why is it so hard for "Christians" to accept Christ is moving "supernaturally" in the lives of believers today?

Now I've seen some ministries where they wanted to wait on the Lord *so* much that nothing ever got done. There is a tension here, where one is trusting and waiting on the Lord, but at the same time, steps need to be taken through the doors the Lord is opening. There is a partnership in ministry – God and us. Cool, huh?

In doing inner-city ministry, one has to totally rely on Christ and seek Him and where He is going. At the same time, they have to have the "gumption" to go all out. Unlike doing ministry in the confines of the church, inner-city ministry does not have a one, two, three step for doing things. They are usually a new ministry. There are many inner-city ministries across the states that have been working with the Lord for many years, such as the Baptist Mission Centers in Houston, and Uptown Baptist Church in Chicago. The need of reaching these young people is great and there are many areas where there is no witness. One does not have to live in a mega-city to have an inner-city ministry. Ask the Lord to open your eyes to see the needs in your town. What are the

---

[19] Proverbs 3:5-6, (New International Version).
[20] Philippians 3:13

opportunities available to minister to the "down and out?" What is the Lord doing?

Now, how should we react to the Lordship of Christ? Let me tell you a story. October 23rd, 1983, General Kelly, the Commandant of the United States Marine Corps was in Beirut, Lebanon, visiting soldiers who were wounded in a terrorist suicide bombing which killed 241 U.S. troops. He was going from bed to bed, pinning on Purple Hearts. He came to one soldier who had more tubes coming out of him that he had ever seen before. General Kelly walked up to the young man who was apparently innocuous and pinned on the Purple Heart. As he turned away to leave, the young man tried to say something. This would probably be the only time that he would come face-to-face and actually speak to his Commander. With tubes running in and out of his nose and mouth, it was impossible for him to speak. Quickly, a bystander brought a pad and pen and held the shaking hand so that the young man could write. He wrote two Latin words, "Semper Fi." Tears filled the eyes of the Marine commander and a lump came into his throat as he told the news correspondent that the soldier had just written in abbreviated form the Marine Corps motto, "Semper Fidelas, " which means, "always faithful."[21] Give you an idea?

---

[21] Kenny Lewis, Sermon delivered at First Baptist Church, Brownsville, Texas, July 2, 1989.

Chapter Four: The Young People

WHY JOIN A GANG?

Red rags are here and blue rags are there
Folks wear them just for a stare.
Extra large T-shirts and big baggy pants
Trying to get a job, but there is no chance.
Lowriders here, loud music there
Gangsters just do that so folks will stare.
Smoking weed and dealing dope
I feel sorry for those people because there is no hope,
They can fight, but it ain't cool
'Cause is makes you look like a fool.
Sometimes I wonder why folks join gangs
'Cause getting into a gang ain't no big of a thing.

Billy Joe Perales

So far, we've talked about several different things which are crucial in ministering to inner-city young people. By far, the most crucial is the young people themselves. Each one is unique and special. They each add a different ingredient to the pot. Each one has hurts, needs, failures, celebrations, and triumphs. They are human beings whom God loved so much that He gave up His own son on their behalf.[22]

First of all, they are hungry! And it's not for meat and potatoes, either. It is for love and acceptance. A void is in

---

[22] Romans 5:8

their lives which can *only* be filled by Christ. They try to fill this "hole" with sex, drugs, gangs, money, power, etc. Sound familiar? People of all races, social status, and age face the same dilemma. We were *all* created with a need for Him. It reminds me of a toy I had when I was a young boy. It was kind of like a tool bench where one hammers a peg through a hole in the bench. Now, the pegs had different shapes with holes that matched. Too many people out there are trying to fill a void in their lives (which can *only* be filled with Christ) with things of this world, which is just like one trying to put a square peg into a round hole.

When they don't find love and acceptance at home, they'll look in other directions. Many times, they'll find this acceptance in the gangs. Thus, the gangs become their new family. Now, another reason young people join gangs is because of peer pressure and not enough positive role models at home to look up to. It looks cool to be in the gangs. The gang members are looked up to by the younger kids.

In many ways, they are not any different from any other youth. A good friend of mine made a comment once that youth are a "very unusual sub-species." That is true to a certain extent. Teenagers are going through a time period where they are too old to be considered children and too young to be considered adults. It is a difficult time in one's life. There are many developments which are happening in their lives: physically, emotionally, mentally, socially, and spiritually.

When puberty hits, an alarm clock goes off and a complex set of biological and chemical changes happen in a person's body that mark the end of childhood and the beginning of the transition from childhood toward adulthood.[23] Here, one's body starts to change in many ways. How one handles these changes is important. It can lead to many different outcomes. Often, inner-city youth have much "freedom." They can go anywhere, anytime they want without much adult supervision. It amazes me how so many youth become sexually active as soon as their hormones become active. In Fort Worth, I would pray that the Lord would protect the young girls as they were entering womanhood. We had one seventeen-year-old boy who had a ten-month-old baby by one girl, a nine-month-old by another girl, and another one on the way by a third mom. Every time a friend from the seminary came by to spend time with them, one question would always come up, "Are you a virgin?" Waiting until marriage for sex was a whole new concept.

During the teenage years, youth change emotionally and mentally. These are usually tough times on the parents as well. The youth's emotions sometimes resemble roller-coasters. Teenagers experience new feelings, and they often do not know how to respond. As a result, emotions can create problems for the young person and anyone around them.[24] We had one youth in Fort Worth that seemed to have a male version of PMS. One second, he was having a great time, then BOOM!, he would explode. As adults who have the privilege of working with youth, or parents, we should always remember Proverbs 15:1, "A gentle answer turns away wrath, but a harsh word stirs up anger."[25]

---

[23] Wesley Black, <u>An Introduction to Youth Ministry</u> (Nashville, Tennessee: Broadman Press, 1991). P. 88.

[24] Wesley Black, <u>An Introduction to Youth Ministry</u> (Nashville, Tennessee: Broadman Press, 1991). p. 91.

[25] The Bible (New International Version).

It is during the teenage years that their social scene also changes. No longer do mom and dad know all of their children's friends. No longer do they know where their child is and what the child is doing at all times. It is during this time that the youth is seeking more freedom and their peers become a 'major" part of their lives. It never ceases to amaze me that when I plan something (even something they have been asking for,) they will wait to the last second to commit to see what everyone else is doing at that moment. Close friends allow teenagers the opportunities to express intimate fears and joys. They play a vital part in the development of the youth.[26]

Just like every other area in their lives, youth grow spiritually, too. Youth must learn to love and be loved by God. They must channel their new emotions in appropriate ways toward loving God, other people, and themselves. It is amazing to see youth who start off "hard" to the Gospel slowly turn and eventually accept Christ's saving grace.[27] In Fort Worth, there was a youth named David. When he first started coming to Teen Club, he was against anything Christian. He would come and play pool, basketball, foosball, etc., but as soon as the Bible time would begin, he would leave. This went on for months, but one day as a friend of mine came to share with the youth, something happened. As usual, David started to the door, but this time, he stopped at the door and stayed. From that moment on, I saw the Lord bring him in closer and his interest increased. He was always coming up with some fantastic questions as he struggles to find the Truth. About a year and a half after he stopped at that

---

[26] Wesley Black, <u>An Introduction to Youth Ministry</u> (Nashville, Tennessee: Broadman Press, 1991). P. 91-99.
[27] Ibid. p. 107-111.

door, he prayed to accept Christ as Lord. *WHOOP!* **Thank You, Jesus!**

Now, just like everyone, youth respond to the Gospel in different ways. As David started out hostile to the message of Christ, Julio and Servando were always there, attentive and wanting to know more. With them, I saw a seriousness for Christ. For two years, they were faithful in coming to the Center to "hang out" and embrace the love of Christ. Now, they did not want to accept Christ until they could fully know it was real. I respected that. I will never forget the day that they came into the FAMILY. That night, I got to see the Lord bring five of my "home boys" (friends) to accept Christ as Savior of their lives.. **PRAISE GOD…WHOOP!**

As I have said before, inner-city youth are not much different than any other youth. Now, what brings out the difference is the environment in which they grow. The youth and children that I have had the privilege to work with grew up in a totally different set of circumstances than where I grew up. One's environment, family, friends, and other influences are like ingredients of a cake. In a cake, each ingredient affects the final product. Let's say we put in salt instead of sugar or totally leave out any yeast. These things will drastically change the outcome of the cake. But what is great is that if one will allow Christ to come in and impact their life, He can change it forever.

One thing that I have found out while working with Hispanic communities is that there is a family tie. Brothers and sisters take up for on another. Even cousins are very close and will fight for one another. Family ties are strong. It might not look that way at first from the outside, but they are. Plus, when one shows interest in the welfare of someone's child or teenager, it usually opens the door for ministry to the rest of the family. Just about everyone likes it when one appreciates their son or daughter.

At this moment, let's ask the Lord to change the stereotypes we have of inner-city youth. That He will take whatever fears or indifference in our lives and transform our lives where we can see others as He sees them. Let's also pray for those in the inner-cities, that the Lord will bring a mighty revival out of the heart of the cities. Believe me, **HE CAN DO IT.**

Chapter Five: The Ministry - Meeting Needs

"One day God had nothing better to do…so with His mighty arms, He reached down into the pit of hell and searched for the ugliest and filthiest thing He could find. He plucked me out with His mighty hand, washed me with the blood of Jesus and said, 'Go and tell them what I did for them.'"

Jose Castillo – Chaplain Coordinator

Baptist Children Home Ministries

San Antonio, Texas- September, 1997

We have talked about the problem, the inner-city culture, letting God be in total control, and also we've talked about the young people themselves. Now, let us talk about the ministry. A lot of times, people like to put down a step-by-step method to do a successful ministry. That's where we're doing things in our own strength and by our own agenda. In this chapter, we are going to talk about an important issue in ministering to inner-city young people – meeting needs.

To begin with, one should take time to get to know the ins and outs of the community. Do not go in blind and stay blind. I once heard a story about some missionaries in South America. They came down and the first thing they did was build a church. It was a little North American church. It was nice and well-constructed, but no one would come to church. It was like pulling teeth. No one even wanted to come close to the building. This had the missionaries really baffled. They did not know what was going on. The problem was this: the people believed that demons lived in corners. That is why they lived in circular homes. If the missionaries would have gotten to know the people first, they might not have made this mistake[28] In the same way, we need to go as a learner and seek the Lord in determining how we should minister to the community.

One thing that I have found out through the years in the Lord's ministry is that we need to be meeting needs. Meeting needs is a must in the life of a Christian. To prove my point, let us find in our Bibles the twenty-fifth chapter of Matthew. I think I need to mention that the way I intend to share this was influenced by a song written by Keith Green, "Sheep and Goats." In this passage, Jesus is telling the disciples about the "end times." He said that when He comes in His glory with all the angels, He will separate all the peoples of the world like a shepherd separates the sheep from the goats. He will put the sheep on His right and the goats on His left.

At that time, the King will say to those on His right, "Come, you are blessed by My Father, take your inheritance, the Kingdom created for you since the creation of the world. I was hungry, you gave Me something to eat. I was thirsty, you gave Me something to drink. I was a stranger, you welcomed me into your home. I was in need of clothes, you clothed me. I was sick, you took care of Me, and when I was in prison, you came to visit Me."

Then the righteous will answer Him, "Lord, when did we see You hungry, and feed You, or thirsty and give You

---

[28] Dwight Hendricks, Illustration in a Bible study, delivered the summer of 1989.

something to drink? When did we see You a stranger and invite You in, or in need of clothes and provide You with clothes? When were you sick and I took care of You; or in prison and I visited you?'

At this, the King will reply, 'I tell you the truth, whatever you did for one of the least of these brothers of mine, you did for Me.'

Then the King will turn to those on his left, 'Depart from me, you who are cursed, into the eternal flames prepared for the devil and his angels. For I was hungry and you gave Me nothing to eat, I was thirsty and you gave Me nothing to drink, I was a stranger and you told Me to go away, I was in need of clothes out in the cold and you turned Me away, I was sick you did not take care of Me; and I was in prison and you did not visit Me.'

They also will answer, 'Lord, when did we ever see You hungry and did not give You something to eat; or thirsty and did not give You something to drink? When were You a stranger and we did not let You in? You weren't one of those creepy people who would come to the door, were You? That is not fair. That is not even our ministry. We did not feel led. Lord, when were You in need of clothing and we did not clothe You? That is not fair either. We did not know what size You wore. Lord, when were You sick and we did not take care of You; or in prison, and did not visit You. When, Lord, when?"

And the King will reply, 'I tell you the truth, whatever you do not do for one of the least of these, you do not do for Me.'

Then they will go away to eternal punishment, but the righteous to eternal life." According to the Scriptures, the only difference between the sheep and the goats is what they *did* and *did not* do![29]

When I was attending East Texas Baptist University, there was a man in Administration that truly had my respect. His name was Pat. Actually, the Lord used him to get me to attend E.T.B.U. because I did not want to go there. Pat was head of the Department of Development. He was always there for people and his door was always open. I am honored to call him my friend.

Once a good friend of mine shared with me that she was not going to be permitted to come back and finish her last two semesters because of financial reasons. Financial Aid had told her that they couldn't help her, because no funds were available. Before the semester started, she came to town to visit friends. While she was there, I took her to see Pat. Before she could finish telling Pat the whole story, Pat got on the phone and opened a door so that she could finish school. Pat was always able to look past the "red tape" and see the need.

In the second chapter of Philippians, the apostle Paul writes, "Do nothing out of selfish ambition or vain conceit, but in humility consider others better than yourselves. Each of you should look not only to your own interests, but also to the interests of others. Your attitude should be the same as that of Christ Jesus: Who, being in very nature God, did not consider equality with God something to be grasped, but made Himself nothing, taking the very nature of a servant, being made in human likeness. And being found in appearance as a man, He

---

[29] Matthew 25:31-46.

humbled Himself and became obedient to death – even death on a cross![30]

The gospel of Mark recalls a statement of Christ (the stuff written in red ink!) where Christ says: "For even the Son of Man did not come to be served, but to serve, and to give his life as a ransom for many."[31]

From the beginning, Christ loved us **so** much that He gave up everything in heaven to come down as a human. He didn't come down and gloat His glory but served others in love and mercy. We are called to the same ministry of servanthood to others. In this way, they can recognize His glory and come under his saving grace. This is not for our glorification, but His. We get the joy of seeing Him ministering to others and changing their lives. But that is not all. Our lives are changed also. The Lord blesses us in such a way, it is indescribable much of the time. You just want to say, **"WOW!"**

Let me put it another way. I have always heard that a child spells love, "T-I-M-E." We can tell people of Christ's love and that we care for them, but it means nothing if we do not show them. We are the only Jesus some people will ever see. It is like if a guy were married and he always told his wife that he loved her, but he never took her anywhere , never did anything special for her, and never held her close. Do you think that she would believe him? His actions speak louder than his words. Our actions speak louder than our words, too.

I feel that I often need to ask the Lord to open my eyes that I may see the needs of others. If I do not, it is too easy to concentrate on my own needs and wants. If I go too long that

---

[30] Philippians 2:3-8, (New International Version).
[31] Mark 10:45, (New International Version).

way, I feel that I become selfish. Please take time now and ask the Lord to open your eyes so you can see the needs of others and how the Lord wants to use us in ministering to them.

Chapter Six: The Ministry - Evangelism

I SLEEP NOW

I sleep now, so don't try to wake me,
The angels are here and they are going to take me.

Looking up in the sky and there you would see my face,
Smiling at you, with such love and grace.

I sleep now, so don't try to wake me,
'Cause the angels are here and now they're gonna take me.

Hear the song, the sweet song of rejoice,
Listen closely and then you'll hear my voice.

I sleep now, so don't try to wake me,
'Cause my sweet Lord Jesus Christ is here now to take me.

Billy Joe Perales

In this chapter, we are going to address another issue which is critical in doing inner-city ministry. Evangelism, right. I know it's an obvious issue, but I feel it still needs to be addressed. Sometimes, we can get so enthused with evangelism that we almost force the witnessee into accepting Christ, while others can go the other extreme where the ministry becomes more like baby-sitting rather than ministry.

In this chapter, we'll discuss the importance of evangelism and what seems to work best in working in the inner-city.

In the past, when one would think of evangelism, they would think of Evangelism Explosion, CWT, 4 Spiritual Laws, etc. Point blank evangelism. Share Christ and part ways. Or one might think of mass evangelism such as the Billy Graham Crusades where thousands of people walk forward in response to the Holy Spirit during a worship service. Now, all these ways are used by the Lord and many people have come into the Family through these means. Over the last several years in working with inner-city ministries, I have found out that these mean work, but relationship evangelism is by far the best method.

You might ask, "What in the world is relationship evangelism?" The *Scribner-Bantam English Dictionary* says that a "relationship" is a connection or involvement. I knew what involvement meant, but I wasn't too sure about connection, so I looked it up. It means, "a transfer to another." So one could say that relationship evangelism is sharing the Good News of Jesus Christ by means of personally getting involved in someone's life.[32]

Now, what about the word, "evangelism?" What does it mean? We hear it all the time in church, ministry groups, para-church organizations such as Campus Crusades, Baptist Student Ministries, Fellowship of Christian Athletes, etc., but what does it actually mean? Evangelism is the first step of a larger process called, "making a disciple." Evangelism means the proclamation by word and deed that Jesus Christ is God and Savior to the end so all men and women can accept Him.

---

[32] Edwin B. Williams, The Scribner-Bantam English Dictionary (Toronto: Bantam Books: 1985), p. 191, 763.

The Bible states in the book of Acts, "Salvation is found in no one else, for there is no other name under heaven given to men by which we must be saved."[33] The name in which is being talked about here is Jesus Christ's. There is no salvation in Mohammad, or Buddha, or the Virgin of Guadeloupe, of in any pastor's name, either. Jesus is the **only** way! It's not a brain washing. It's a simple sharing of God's love for mankind. A free gift of having a relationship with one's Creator, the One Almighty God.

When you really think about it, it's really exciting. Because God could easily *zap* everybody and they'd be Christians, but He loves us so much that He decided to share that joy and excitement of someone coming into the FAMILY with us.

In relationship evangelism, one shows the other that they are important and special. That they are worth the time to get to know and experience life together. Inner-city young people don't automatically give someone their complete trust. They would like to, but the streets have taught them differently. The neighborhood I had the privilege of ministering in Ft. Worth is known as "Rock Island." There is a myth there that there are **no** friends in Rock Island. ***Watch who you trust, 'cause they let you down or they will turn on you.*** I got the honor of seeing the Lord blow this "myth" away. But the idea is still true, it's a part of life. One earns the "right" to share Christ. A trust has to be developed. They want to believe, but at the same time, they want to make sure it's real.

They want to know if Jesus makes a difference in your life. Is this Jesus just lip service or can He make an impact on their lives? They will look to you for these answers. They will

---

[33] Acts 4:12, (New International Version).

watch how you act and respond in different situations. They will look to see if you genuinely care and they will judge Christianity by your actions.

There are two big ingredients in relationship evangelism: being real and being vulnerable. These two aspects go hand-in-hand because when one is real, they makes themselves vulnerable. When ones does this, they open themselves up and show that they care. It's amazing that when one becomes open, people become more comfortable and open themselves up, too.

The outcome of openness and trust is not a product of ourselves, but it's from our Lord Jesus Christ. The closer we allow ourselves to get to God and love others as Christ loves us creates a better atmosphere for the Lord to do His stuff! If we don't, we end up quenching the Holy Spirit and will not receive the blessing of seeing God move in a person's life.

I know, I know, you're asking, "What blessing?" Man, there's a hunk of blessing just waiting for you. The greatest joy, the greatest experiences I have ever experienced in my life is seeing God bring someone into the family. It makes you want to say, "Wow!" Then you get so excited that you say it backwards, "Wow!" Then you get even more excited where you say it upside down, "Mom!" When you see the Creator of the universe, who placed each star in its place, reach down and embrace an individual into the Family—it's just indescribable.

John was a youth that started to come to Teen Club one summer. Teen Club was a place where the teens could come down to the community center to "hang out." Here they could come and play basketball, pool, foosball, ping pong, fellowship, and embrace the love of Christ. He started to show up and about a month and a half later I was able to call him my brother. I was on cloud nine. I was so excited to see someone I cared about rescued from the pain and suffering of hell.

We started looking at the Bible together to find out what God says about Himself in His word. It was exciting to see him grow. At the time he was living with his girlfriend and her family. She was pregnant and he felt that he needed to do the right thing and he married the one he loved. I was honored to be invited to their wedding and when the beautiful little girl was born, we (Teen Club) were their first stop from the hospital.

My first ministry position after college was up in Southern Idaho. There I was a Minister of Youth in a town of 2,800 people. Half of them were Mormon, so this made things very interesting. While I was there I met a teen named Dustin while playing a pick up football in a vacant lot. While I was there it seemed that the Lord was constantly taking me to the ones that no one wanted to deal with. If one was blonde haired, blue eyed, and clean cut, then there was a good chance that they were Mormon. The guys the Lord took me to had long dark hair, tattoos, smoked, and visited the court systems regularly. Dustin was one of these guys and the Lord developed a friendship between us. About three months of cultivating a friendship and sharing Christ with him, he accepted the calling that the Holy Spirit was laying on his heart. **WHOOP!**

What was sad, after the Lord took me back to Texas, Dustin started to get back in trouble with the law. A good friend in the ministry named Bob met with Dustin in jail and got word back to me that he was hanging on to his faith and wanted to get his life right. Dustin is still having problems resisting the world and following Jesus completely. Hey, we all have that same problem too, so don't look down on him. He's a special young man.

While I attended Blinn Junior College (5 years part time) trying to get into Texas A&M University, I was able to attend the Baptist Student Ministry. It was one of the greatest times of my life. It was a time where the Lord used the B.S.M. to disciple me and teach me about missions. The director of the B.S.M. was Mike. The Lord used him in a big way in a lot of lives. One thing I'll never forget is that he always stressed and challenged us to invest our lives in that which is eternal. There are only two things in this world that are eternal— God's Word (the Bible) and people's souls.

Let's take time out and ask the Lord to give us a heart to put His Word in our hearts (Psalms 119:11) and a burden for the salvation of others. When you think about it, when we don't share Christ with others, we are basically telling them to go to hell.

Chapter Seven: The Ministry - Discipleship

As I stated before, evangelism isn't the final product. It's just the first step of a great experience of life. Too many times we stop after there is a salvation experience, but this isn't right. That's just like going through a complete pregnancy and immediately after the birth, to send the baby into the world to get a job and make a living for itself. We are doing the same thing when we don't disciple.

A lot of times, people accept Christ, get baptized, and fall into the cracks of the church. The next thing you know they've joined a cult, a false religion, or something. They don't do this because they reject Christ, but because they were not given a chance to grow in their new relationship with Christ.

Right before Jesus ascended up to heaven, Jesus gave what is now known as the "Great Commission:"

"Then Jesus came to them and said, 'All authority in heaven and earth has been given to Me. Therefore go and make disciples of all nations, baptizing them in the name of the Father, and of the Son, and of the Holy Spirit, and teaching them to obey everything I have commanded you. And surely I will be with you to the end of the age."[34]

Now, there are several things that I would like to point out about what Jesus says here. First, you notice that He says, "...make disciples of all nations." Dr. Ebbie C. Smith of Southwestern Baptist Seminary, calls the process of discipleship, "effective evangelism." The goal to "effective evangelism" or discipleship is to seek followers instead of decisions.[35] A disciple of Christ is a follower of Christ. Here they can grow in the Lord where they can be used to make an impact on the world. It's kind of like a shampoo commercial which was popular when I was growing up. The girl on the commercial said that she enjoyed the product so much that she told two friends, and they told two friends, and so on, and so on, and so on. There is a multiplication of the ministry instead of an addition to. The second thing that I would like to mention is that this is a command, not an option. In the military, they call it as "standing order." That is where the

---

[34] Matthew 28: 18-20, (New International Version).
[35] Ebbie C. Smith, Balance Church Growth, (Nashville: Broadman Press, 1984), p. 38.

order stands until the commander gives a new order, and THE COMMANDER hasn't done that. The last thing that I would like to bring up about this text is the last part, "And surely I will be with you to the end of the age." This command is not supposed to weigh us down and twist us into the ground. Instead, He promises us that He will be right there with us, seeing us through. He takes the weight off our shoulders. Isn't that great or what?

One might think that discipleship is a New Testament principle, but it's really not. Let me give you an example. During the times of the "Divided Kingdoms," there was a king over Judah named Amon. Now Amon did evil in the eyes of the Lord like his father, Manasseh. He worshipped idols and followed the ways of his father. He reigned in Jerusalem just two years. His sins caught up to him. After Amon's assassination his son Josiah was made king.[36]

Now get this, Josiah was just eight years old when he became king. Can you imagine being a king at the age of eight? The responsibilities, the pressures, the stress must have been enormous. Now in the eighteenth year of his reign as king of Judah, Hilkam, the high priest found the Book of the Law which had apparently been misplaced for many years. This is probably the "Pentitude," (the first five books of the Bible) which was written by Moses. This was brought to Josiah and read to him. When the king heard what was read from the Book he tore his robes (because he realized that the nation of Israel had sinned against the Lord) and asked Hilkah to go and inquire of the Lord about what was heard. You see, the nation of Israel and their fathers didn't obey what the Lord had told them and His anger was great. God was ready to punish the nation of Israel for their many sins,

---

[36] II Kings 21: 19-26.

but He decided not to because Josiah's heart was responsive and he humbled himself before the Lord. Josiah led the nation to renew their covenant or commitment to the Lord. Josiah also got rid of the mediums and spiritists, the household gods, the idols, and all the other detestable things seen in Judah and Jerusalem. This was a radical turn around for the nation. God had brought a revival, a renewal, reconciliation with His chosen people.[37]

Now get this. This is very important. Both Josiah's grandfather, Manasseh, and his father, Amon, did evil in the eyes of the Lord. They followed other gods and did as they please. How in the world did Josiah turn out different? As an eight year old king, I'm sure he had advisors who taught him the ropes. In my opinion the "Gospel according to Brian," a godly mother and a high priest named Hilkah raised him in the ways of the Lord. This made a BIG impact on him that affected his whole life. At the end of Josiah's life, this was written about him: "Neither before nor after Josiah was there a king like him who turned to the LORD as he did ---- with all his heart and all his soul and all his strength, in accordance with all the Law of Moses."[38] What a statement! That includes King David who God calls, "a man after his own heart." That's BIG!

I remember when I was growing up, discipleship was offered Sunday afternoon before church. This has been called Training Union and Discipleship Training. It was offered and I believe still is offered in a classroom or group environment. To me I was not interested. It was boring. It gave the attitude that discipleship was not *that* important. It was an option. That's not biblical!

---

[37] II Kings 22-23:30.
[38] II Kings 23:25 (New International Version).

I believe that discipleship works best in the midst of a relationship. This is where you learn in a mentor/learner atmosphere. This is how Jesus taught the disciples. Yes, He taught multitudes in a so-on-so "classroom" atmosphere, but He took "the Twelve" off and taught them separately. He taught them by sharing his life. Can you imagine what it was like walking down those dusty roads learning from, singing, and joking around with Jesus. **Son!**

When I was serving down in Brownsville, we would take kids who were excited about Jesus and would meet with them once a week. This was a very special time which I looked forward to. It was a time that I was able to get to know the kids and I got to see the Lord move miraculously in many different was each day. It was awesome! God was in control and we went by His agenda. Down on San Pablo St. the Lord gave me the privilege of discipling John, Jose, and Saul for three summers. These were very memorable times. I would have to say that John and Jose were two of the most ticklish kids in the northern hemisphere. During these times, not only was I able to see them grow in the Lord and minister to them, but I got a chance to be used in the ministry towards their families too. John and Jose's mom had terminal cancer. She was so supportive. She knew that she was dying and all she wanted was for her family to follow God. I was able to be an extension of God's grace to that family. I wonder how they are doing now... *Lord, please take care of them.*

In Ft. Worth, the Lord brought Joey across my path. Joey would come to Teen Club, play basketball, listen to the lesson and go on his way. He was a member of the Baptist church down the street and was open to "spiritual" things. We became friends and I began to "assume" that he knew the Lord in a personal way. WRONG! The Lord has always been trying to teach me to never assume. These are human lives...people...that we are dealing with. I was asked to teach the youth class at the church's Vacation Bible School one summer and Joey prayed to accept Christ as his Lord and Savior on the tailgate of my truck. **WHOOP!**

After Joey accepted Christ, we bought him a Bible and started to search the Scriptures to find out what God says about Himself. We looked to see what the Bible said on who God the Father, Son, and Holy Spirit was and how we relate to Him. It is exciting to see the Lord move in the life of others.

During this time we were able to take some youth with a church group to Youth Camp and Joey went. Along with his friend Juan, they both learned a lot about what it means to follow Christ and got a lot of fishing done. The last night at the end of the service, John came down to the front. We walked out to the pier that overlooked the lake. With tears coming out of his eyes, John shared his desire to know God more. John has been a friend whom I have been able to go to for prayer and we've continued our discipleship. Both Joey and John have taken advantage of special opportunities to grow in his relationship with the **ONE** and **ONLY GOD** of the universe. They took some teasing for their stands for the Lord, but many of those who did the teasing now know the Lord. I believe that the Lord used Joey in bringing them into the Family.

Let us not get caught up in evangelism in such a way where we leave off discipleship. They go hand in hand. Let's ask the Lord to show us the importance and joy in discipleship. *Lord, please use us in Your ministry of bringing people back to You.*

Chapter Eight: The Ministry -Intervention And Prevention

GENERATION OF HATE

This is a generation of hate,
Where my homeboys are dying at a great rate
'Cause my homeboy has passed away,
on this certain day
So that we can see him at his grave,
'cause he was so brave
And now I won't see him wave,
'cause too many things lead to his going astray
We're shocked at his morals, amazed at his crimes,
My homeboy lived in such dangerous times.

Billy Joe Perales

During my last semester of seminary, I took a mentoring course. This here was a FANTASTIC course to take, because you learned while doing ministry and learned from someone out there in the ministry. The mentor I chose was a guy named David. David was in a Latino gang in Chicago when he accepted Christ as Lord. The Lord has been using David in a BIG way in gang intervention and prevention. Much of the following in this chapter is what I learned while doing my mentoring with David.

First of all, what does prevention and intervention mean in the concept of working with inner-city young people? Prevention is where youth live in a gang-infiltrated community and have at-risk characteristics that make them vulnerable to the appeal of a gang lifestyle. This approach is aimed at deterring youth from joining a gang. Intervention is where you on work with hard core gang members who fully participate in the activities of the gang. Intervention is an attempt to reclaim youth from all gang activity. One cannot do prevention without intervention or vice-versa. They are like brother and sister; they go hand-in-hand.[39]

Remember Jesus loves everyone and died for them, too. This concept helps one get in the right mindset before going out. Also, one must be aware of the gangs to which one is ministering. Who are involved in the surrounding neighborhoods? Find out if there is a structure or chain of command in the gang. Each gang is a little bit different, just like families. To retrieve this information, one needs to get out in the community to find out from the youth and contact the local chapter of Boys and Girls Clubs of America.

Their symbols, paraphernalia (clothing, etc.,) colors, language (terminology,) purpose, goals, and the history of the gang need to be understood. Just like it is meaningful to us for them to read and learn from the Bible, it is meaningful to them for us to try to understand what is important to them. It is also important to find out why the gang exists. There are many different reasons gangs exist: money, drugs, protection, identity, etc. This gives a better understanding of them and an idea about how we can relate to them.[40]

Two of the most key elements in working with gangs are building trust and credibility.[41] These are crucial. These are

---

[39] Interview with David Rosario, Fort Worth, Texas, Boys and Girls Club of America, March 27, 1997.
[40] Ibid.
[41] Ibid.

not just handed out on a platter, either. They need to know if you really care and if you are who you say you are. Building trust and credibility is following up and following through with the younger generation. Is your "yes" yes and your "no" no? Do not, I repeat, do not make promises you cannot keep to make a friend. Not only does it discredit you, but it also teaches the other person not to trust others. If they cannot trust in others, then how can they trust in Christ? Get the picture? Your intentions may be good, but be careful.

Two other key elements of intervention/prevention are respect and acceptance for who they are.[42] Many young people enter gangs for acceptance and if we don't accept them, we're just reinforcing their reason for being in the gang. Once, Jesus decided to leave Judea, which was in the southern part of Israel and go back to Galilee which was in the northern part of Israel. Now, the normal path was to travel east across the Jordan River, turn north for a good ways, and then turn back east and cross the Jordan again to enter into Galilee. This route looks kind of like a half of a square. I remember from 10th grade Geometry that the shortest distance between two points is a straight line. What gives? Between Galilee and Judea, there is a place called Samaria. About a thousand years before Christ, the nation of Israel split into a southern kingdom (Judah) and a northern kingdom (Samaria.) Those who lived in the Northern Kingdom were later taken off into bondage where they intermarried and lost their identity. The Samaritans were the descendants of these people. There were considered half-breeds. The Jewish people disliked the Samaritans so much that they would not acknowledge of speak to them. Now, Jesus took the shortest route, straight through Samaria. While doing this, He came

---

[42] Ibid.

across a well. He was worn out by the trip, so he stopped to rest. After a short period of time, a Samaritan woman came to draw water from the well. Jesus asked her for some water and her mouth fell open because He spoke to her. This totally shocked her because not only was she a Samaritan, but also, she was a woman. Women were considered inferior and were not addressed in public. There was a popular prayer by men, "Lord, thank You for not making me a Samaritan, a woman, or a dog."[43] She then asked Him why he was speaking to her and He answered that He could give her "living water." She quickly ran back to town and told people about the great Man she met. At the end, many Samaritans came to believe in Jesus and accepted Him as Lord.[44] Jesus showed respect to the woman and accepted her for *who* she was – a human being in need of a Savior.

In dealing with inner-city youth or anyone else, it is important to be bold and truthful. In doing this, you show them that it is important and an honor to help lead the youth out of the cycle of violence and poverty.[45] It shows them that they are important. We need to break the cycle of fear in the lives of the "mainstream." Instead, let us open our eyes so we can see creative ways of ministry. Offering job opportunities where youth are able to learn job skills and self-respect is one avenue of ministry. There are also grants and scholarships providing opportunities for them to earn degrees and to have experiences they would not normally have.

---

[43] Lecture by Dr. Bruce Tankersley, Professor of Religion, East Texas Baptist University, Fall of 1990.

[44] John 4:1-42.

[45] Interview with David Rosario, Fort Worth, Texas, Boys and Girls Club of America, March 27, 1997.

In Fort Worth, the Lord used the city council to provide an eighteen to twenty-one thousand dollar grant to build a concrete basketball court with lights. And this was without **any** restrictions. **Can God cook or what?** This court was the showcase of the neighborhood and it was like a flint rock to spark the youths' interests. The Lord has continued to use that court to bring in the neighborhood youth where they have been able to embrace God's saving grace.

It seems that those in the "mainstream" and business sections of our communities have a specific stereotype of these young people – "high risk." For this reason, many are not given opportunities of employment. There is a great resource out there, which has yet to be tapped. It seems that we can only think of the negative images we see on the news and read about in the newspaper. We do not realize the potential that they have to offer. One can find persistence, endurance, determination and courage in these young people. It is a matter of survival. There is also a strong sense of loyalty to those who are loyal to them, a sense of unity and a need to belong. There is a ton of untapped talent out there, if someone would invest time to look. Among the young people, one can find a sense of remorse and understanding also. In the more structured gangs, one can find those who are used to receiving and carrying out orders, too.[46] Aren't those qualities that one looks for in employees?

This seemed more like a game than anything, but it's very important. You must use your head and be alert to what is happening at all times. This is not just to watch your back, but you're also watching out for them.[47] When one is working in the inner-cities, one needs to be aware of what is happening

---

[46] Ibid.
[47] Ibid.

around them. This is one thing that they will be studying about you. A lot of times, we have had a youth act like they were going to steal an object just to see if we were paying attention or noticed it.

Another aspect that I have found that is very important is giving responsibility. Give them responsibility and the trust to get the job done. We all love it when someone has confidence in us. It's eaten up! We had a youth in Fort Worth who thrived on being responsible. Give him something to do, mixed in with a little guidance and encouragement, and there was no telling what he could do. It wasn't just him, either. I saw others respond in the same way. They are hungry for it.

Do you remember when Jesus went back home to Nazareth, spoke in the synagogue, and was rejected by the people who saw Him grow up. The scripture He read was a passage out of Isaiah:

> "The Spirit of the Lord is on me, because the Lord has anointed me to preach the good news to the poor. He has sent me to bind up the broken-hearted, to proclaim freedom for the captives and release for the prisoners, to proclaim the year of the Lord's favor."[48]

This you could say is Jesus' mission statement. You know, the same is said of us, too, because this sounds like an Old Testament version of the "Great Commission." This is exactly what is being done in intervention and prevention and in inner-city ministries. We are out there ministering to those in grief and hopelessness, providing freedom from the bondage of sin and violence, and the ministry of reconciliation. It is an awesome thought to know that the Lord can use us as He

---

[48] Luke 4:18-19, Isaiah 61:1-2.

continues to bring others to Himself. Please take this time to ask the Lord to bind up the spirit of fear so He can possibly use you in some form or fashion in ministering to the inner-cities.

Chapter Nine: The Ministry - It Takes The Whole Body

Too many times, I've heard the old saying, "If you want something done right, you've got to do it yourself." In the ministry, this is a false statement. Sometimes, it is hard for me to get this idea out of my head. I admit it. Sometimes, I know just how a situation needs to be handled, so I just do it myself. Too many times, I believe ministers have fallen into the same trap and too many times, the Church allows this situation to happen.

I believe that we have professionalized the ministry **so** much that we put ministers on a "spiritual pedestal" – a lot higher than a regular, pew-sittin' Christian. We kind of perceive that there is a hierarchy ladder of spirituality: the foreign missionary is on top, then comes the denominational leaders, pastors, educational directors, college and youth ministers, and then the layman. It's the minister's "job" to do the ministry. **WRONG!!!** We are **all** called to do ministry. Everyone who calls Christ "Lord," is to be a minister. There is no excuse. We are all on the same level. We need to allow the Lord to use us as He sees fit.

I remember when I was a kid, when I went to my grandparents' house, I was able to watch *The Lone Ranger* on television. I can still remember the music and seeing him riding his white horse, Silver, across the screen. With only Tonto, his trusted sidekick, the Lone Ranger was on a solo mission to bring justice across the Old West. It seemed that he would come in, catch the bad guys, save the day, leave his "signature" silver bullet, and ride off with the heroine asking, "Who was that masked man?" It makes a great story; but in the ministry, it leads to stress, burnout, and missed opportunities.

The apostle Paul addresses this issue in his first letter to the church in Corinth:

> "The body is a unit, though it is made up of many parts; and though all its parts are many, they form one body. So it is with Christ. For we were all baptized by one Spirit into one body–whether Jews or Greeks, slave or free, *(minister or layman)* –and we were all given the one Spirit to drink.
>
> Now the body is not made up of one part but of many. If the foot should say, "Because I am not a hand, I do not belong to the body," it would not for that reason cease to be part of the body. And if the ear should say, "Because I am not an eye, I do not belong to the body," it would not

for that reason cease to be part of the body. If the whole body were an eye, where would the sense of hearing be? If the whole body were an ear, where would the sense of smell be? But in fact God has arranged the parts in the body, every one of them, just as he wanted them to be. If they were all one part, where would the body be? As it is, there are many parts, but one body.

The eye cannot say to the hand, "I don't need you!" And the head cannot say to the feet, "I don't need you!" On the contrary, those parts of the body that seem to be weaker are indispensable, and the parts that we think are less honorable we treat with special honor. And the parts that are unpresentable are treated with special modesty, while our presentable parts need no special treatment. But God has combined the members of the body and has given greater honor to the parts that lacked it, so that there should be no division in the body, but that its parts should have equal concern for each other. If one part suffers, every part suffers with it; if one part is honored, every part rejoices with it.

Now you are the body of Christ, and each one of you is a part of it."[49]

Now, let's take a look at the above text. The first thing that stands out is that we are all baptized by the same Spirit – the Holy Spirit. **All** Christians are given the same Spirit, the same salvation, the same freedom, and the same power. This includes the pew   sitters and even the children and the youth. They are not *just* the future of the Church, but **they are the Church today**, too!

---

[49] I Corinthians 12:12-27 (New International Version).

Secondly, people have different gifts and talents in the Church. Paul uses the illustration of the body. Let's say you wake up in bed and you are hungry. Usually, one can just roll over and go back to sleep, but there are times the hunger is too strong. Now, the stomach just can't get out of bed by itself and get something to eat. Other body parts are necessary to accomplish the task of meeting this need. First of all, one needs feet and legs to get across the house to the refrigerator. Ears are needed to control balance and eyes to keep from running into walls. Now you're at the refrigerator, it takes eye-hand coordination and arms and fingers to open the refrigerator door and grab a Ding Dong or something. Now, before the hunger is satisfied, the teeth, tongue, throat, and stomach have to do their part. Each part of the body plays an important part in accomplishing the goal.

Inner-city ministries are no different. They are extensions of the Church. It seems that inner-city ministries have a problem getting by. It seems that many of the churches are not very interested in what happens there. Many of these ministries do not have enough money, materials, and man power. They are constantly in a struggle to keep things going.

Out of every hundred people who answers God's call to do missions, only five make it out on the field. That is not a very good ratio. Satan seems to swoop in like an eagle trying to swipe these Christians away. His main method of doing this is by throwing barriers in the way. Some of these barriers are financial (cannot support a family,) family (fear from the immediate family,) marriage (marrying someone who does not have the same calling,) fear of the environment, being comfortable, language, and many more.[50]

As Christians, we are **ALL** called, the **WHOLE** body, to be a part of His work in calling people back to Himself. Now, this does not mean that every Christian should move to the inner-city or go out and get their visa and go overseas. There are both "goers" and "senders" in God's ultimate plan. They are equally important!

The goers position is one that is seen and is known about. For this reason, I am going to concentrate on the role of the sender. Too many times, we think of the sender role as a passive one. We will pray for the goers on their birthdays or when we hear of a special need. The majority of the times, that is it! As senders, we need to seek to find out how the Lord wants us to be "barrier breakers." We need to help seek funding for those out on the mission field (whether here or abroad,) so they can concentrate on the ministry at hand instead of spending their time figuring out how they will survive. Maybe being consistent in writing letters of encouragement is our role. It's a big lift to find out that someone is praying for you. It might be providing materials for the ministry or opportunities such as sports events so the youth can attend something that normally they would never. Prayer, prayer, and more prayer. There are many different ways .Let's get creative and ask the Lord to use us in whatever way He sees fit. The senders are just as important as the goers. Their role is just as important as if they were right beside the goer sharing Christ.

---

[50] Lecture by Dave Dougherty, Professor of Perspectives, Grace Bible Church, January 17, 1989.

I have always had a problem with delegating. This is an area the Lord has been working on. I know in my head what and how to do it, but it's hard to voice it out. My first summer in Brownsville, Texas, as Dwight's assistant, I had a big problem with this. Dwight would come to me with a task and I would take care of it. After a while, Dwight noticed what was happening and he came to me. He asked me, "How does a man do the work of ten men?" Knowing Dwight, there was something to the question, so I asked how. "Get tem men to do it," he replied. That word of advice has stuck with me till this day. It's a struggle every day, but I try to follow the advice my mentor in the ministry gave me.

If you are a goer, remember that you should not be a "Lone Ranger," but one part of a larger body. If you are not a goer, then you are a sender. Now if that is so, don't be a passive sender, but an active one. We all are a part of one body and one army (the army of God) and there is a mission at hand! Sit back, take a deep breath, and ask the Lord to show you what he would have for you to do.

Chapter Ten: The Ministry - Flexibility

I remember when I first started to get involved in missions was back in college. I learned that the definition of a missionary is "flexibility." No, this does not have anything to do with how limber you are. The dictionary calls is, "adaptable."[51] I've always heard that there is an old Indian saying that the willow is stronger than the oak.[52] There is a lot of truth to that. If a strong wind comes, the oak will break and might even be pulled out of the ground, but the willow on the other hand, will bend with the wind and survive.

---

[51] Edwin B. Williams, <u>The Scribner-Bantam English Dictionary</u> (Toronto: Bantam Books: 1985), p. 347.

[52] Anecdotal incident, source unknown.

In life, things do not always go exactly the way we want it. Ministry is no different. There are times that plans, events, and confrontations fall apart. How should one react? How would you react?

How one responds to certain situations is very crucial. Too many times, we etch our plans in stone and **that's just the way we are going to do it.** We have to realize Who is in control. It goes back to Lordship and what we discussed in Chapter Three. Jesus is Lord of ALL! This includes ALL that we do and every circumstance we go through.

Back in high school, I was able to see the world in a whole different light. I was diagnosed with an inoperable brain tumor. To make a long story short, the Lord cured me when the doctors gave up on me. It was during this time, the Lord gave me a whole new way of looking at things. Too many times, we let our situations control the way we feel and act. We can let things that are really not important ruin our day. The other day, I was changing lanes while driving. I looked in my side and rearview mirrors before changing lanes. I had a car speeding up in the other lane, but it was still a ways back., so I turned on my directional lights and slowly changed lanes. When the car passed me, the driver "shot the bird" at me while saying some obscenities. All I could do was smile and pray for him. We need to see what is **really** important in life and not get so stressed out on the others.

The Bible says that we should give thanks in all circumstances and consider it pure joy when we face trials. Paul writes in his first letter to the church of the Thessalonians to be joyful always, continue to pray, and give thanks no matter what. This is God's will for us who are in

Christ Jesus.[53] The writer of the book of James takes it a step further by telling us to consider it pure joy when we face trials.[54] When we face trials, we are forced to totally depend on His strength and that is when things happen. He can do things so much better than what we can do.

During my college career, I had an opportunity to supply preach up in a small town in northeast Texas. The Lord had given me His message for the evening service and not one for the morning service, but I felt comfortable with a sermon that I had done before. I was sitting on the first pew during the worship service waiting for "my" time to share what the Lord had laid on my heart. Halfway through the hymn, before the special music that preceded the sermon, the Lord started to lay on my heart the message that He wanted spoken that morning. Now, you talk about being startled. I reached around the pew that I was sitting in and grabbed an offering envelope. I then scribbled two or three notes on it and then it was time for "the sermon." I started off by stating that the Lord had just laid a message on my heart as I tossed my "prepared" sermon over my shoulder. Now, I did not remember a word that I said, but an elderly lady came to me afterward and told me that it reminded her of a service forty years before. I figured that it must have been really good or really bad. God has His plan and we must align ourselves with His ministry, not the opposite.

Now, it is not always our putting our own plans before God's plans or our misunderstanding of His plans. There is another element of this equation: the ruler of the sky, the prince of darkness, Satan. He is not a little red devil with a pitchfork...he is BIG trouble. Satan is always trying to do

---

[53] I Thessalonians 5:16-18.
[54] James 1:2-4.

whatever it takes to keep people from coming to the Lord. There is a spiritual battle out there. Paul wrote to the Ephesians:

> "For our struggle is not against flesh and blood, but against the rulers, against the authorities, against the powers of this dark world and against the spiritual forces of evil in the heavenly realms."[55]

A battle is raging and we need to be ready.

There were times in Fort Worth that I would be sharing a message with "the guys" after a couple of hours of basketball, foosball, or pool, and someone would ask a question about God that was totally off the subject. Then this would be followed by a couple more. It is the "let us chase the rabbit" game. I played it many times myself in college and seminary. Sometimes, I would let it happen and the Lord would bring it full circle to His message and where He wanted it. **BOOM!** I think it amazed them as much as myself. It was just confirmation of Who was in control.

There are other times when schedules are blown out of the water. There is no need to get upset of stressed out. Just give everything to God and be ready for whatever He opens up. Relax...he's in control. Then pray and look for the Lord to open a door of opportunity. Now, this door does not always have a blinking neon sign on it. Many times, it takes ingenuity and a lot of faith. We need to trust that if we are going down the wrong path, the Lord will direct us into the right direction.

---

[55] Ephesians 6:12 (New International Version).

One of the summers when I was in Brownsville, we had to use both buses and a van to take youth groups witnessing in Mexico. Now, I was driving the van with Henry (Russian major from Texas A & M) who was acting as co-pilot. We were following the buses, but at the border, a national got between us as the buses. Apparently, she had been shopping because the border patrol went through her purchases. While we were waiting our turn, the buses left. They did not realize that we were not behind them. I started to drive in the direction that the buses had gone. We looked down the side streets, but could not find them. At that point, I remembered a neighborhood Dwight had showed us just weeks before where we wanted to take a group witnessing. I almost knew how to get there, I wasn't 100% sure. We took off, anyway. I remember the youth asking if we were lost and I replied, "No, we're not lost. I know exactly where I'm at…Mexico!" Lost is when you do not know where you are going and you do not know how to get back. We knew how to get back. We found the neighborhood and the rest of the group wasn't there. We paused, looked around, then we got out and started sharing Christ. It was an awesome afternoon! I was able to see the Lord bring a mother and a daughter into the Family. In all, we saw six people pray to accept Christ as their Savior. **WHOOP!** When we got lost, we could have easily packed it in and headed back to the center, but we trusted the Lord, kept going, and let the Lord do HIS STUFF! Actually, we never made it out to that community the rest of the summer. Thank You, Lord, for putting that lady in front of us. When we got back, we received some teasing about not being able to find our way around without getting lost. We just replied that we followed the Spirit, not man.

Let us ask the Lord, are we willing to keep going when things start to fall apart? Are we willing to get readjusted and look again at the Lord to see where He's leading? Last, but not least, are we willing to follow?

Chapter Eleven: The Ministry - Prayer

One of the greatest resources we have is prayer...that's right, prayer. Most of the time, we don't really realize how important prayer is. We tend to wait till the last moment when things are falling apart to resort to prayer. I don't know, could it be our pride or could it be that we do not fully understand the power of prayer?

Simply, prayer is communication with the Creator of the universe, who made all that is, has been, and what will be. It is amazing that the One who placed each star in the sky wanted to have a relationship with us. **WOW!** He is there for us in times of sorrow, joy, stress, relaxation, etc.

I don't know why so many people don't fully experience the power of prayer. Maybe it's because there is a lack of faith in our world. When I was involved in the Baptist Student Ministry at Texas A & M University, I remember witnessing to an aerospace engineer major and he could not grasp the idea of faith. For something to be true for him, he has to be able to put it under a microscope and test it. A lot of people are like this and maybe some of this reasoning has drifted into the church.

Jesus told His disciples that with faith the size of a mustard seed, they could move mountains.[56] The mustard seed is a very small seed...about the size of a straight pin head. So what does that say about our faith? **Ouch! That hurts!** We need to have faith that the Lord is powerful enough to answer prayers and meet the needs of his children.

Prayer is vital to missions. Missions and especially inner-city ministries need prayer because they are going right into the "lions' den." Satan is having a party in this world and

---

[56] Matthew 17:20.

whenever there is a beachhead of ministry or Christians letting Christ live through them, he's going to fight back. Paul writes in his letter to the Ephesians:

"Finally, be strong in the Lord and in his mighty power. Put on the full armor of God so that you can take your stand against the devil's schemes. For our struggle is not against flesh and blood, but against the rulers, against the authorities, against the powers of this dark world and against the spiritual forces of evil in the heavenly realms."[57]

There is a spiritual battle out there and we need to be ready. Paul goes on to describe the armor we should wear: belt of truth, breastplate of righteousness, shoes of readiness, shield of faith, helmet of salvation, and the sword of the Spirit (which is the word of God.)[58] Did you notice that this is a pretty complete set of armor? But…there is one thing missing – there is nothing covering the back. There is no retreat in the Lord's Army. That's when we are vulnerable. Now, the verse following this passage says:

"And pray in the spirit on all occasions with all kinds of prayers and requests. Wish this in mind, be alert and always keep on praying for all the saints."[59]

This passage stresses always to be alert and continue to pray. There is a sense of importance here.

Just before the Persian Gulf War, when tension was building and the Allied Forces were building up their arsenal, I saw a portion of a news broadcast where they were talking

---

[57] Ephesians 6:10-12 (New International Version).
[58] Ephesians 6:14-17.
[59] Ephesians 6:18 (New International Version).

about the A-10 bomber. During this report, they alluded to the fact that the infantry's best friend was air support. It was at this time that the Lord shared with me that the best friend of the Army of the Lord is prayer support. God has chosen to work through prayer to glorify Himself. Through prayer, we are putting out dependence on Him and His strength – not our own. There is power in prayer!

Many times, Satan attacks us by making us believe that our prayers are not important. Sometimes, I have caught myself saying about a situation that is out of my hands, "All I can do is pray." **Yuck!** What is wrong with me? The <u>best</u> thing I can do is pray. He can do **so** much more than I can ever imagine. Don't let the Great Deceiver lie to you that you can't do anything about a situation.

I have noticed a difference when I give a time of ministry over to the Lord and His control and when I do it in my own power. It is obvious! Most of the time, I just get so busy that I forget to surrender the time to Him. Afterward, I feel so stupid, but He forgives me and I learn much more about ministry and just how much I need Him. Guard your prayer time. Do not let Satan rob you of that special time.

As a body of believers in the Lord Jesus Christ, we have to realize that we are all called to be witnesses of what Christ has done in our lives. You do not have to be licensed, ordained, or have a seminary degree. He can use you in a big way. Through prayer, you can minister in areas in which you personally could never afford to go. The Lord has blessed me with faithful prayer supporters and I have tried to let them know that they are just as important to the ministry as if they were right there standing next to me. Let us be aggressive prayer warriors. Let us seek how we can lift ministries, ministers, and people up.

Once, a family accepted an appointment to go to the mission field. They told their church that they would only go if they had the prayer support from their home church, which was sending them. The church sent them gladly, vowing that they would be praying for them. A year or so past and a worn-out man quietly slipped in the back door at the beginning of the prayer meeting. No one recognized him, though he did look familiar. There was not one mention of the family and the ministry the church had vowed to support. At the end of the meeting, the man walked up to the front of the church and started to speak. He was the husband of the family that had left for the mission field. He was the only one left. Disease had killed off his family. His only happiness was in the Lord Jesus, but he wanted to know one thing. "Why did you forget us?"

Prayer is so important that the Lord Jesus Christ took a lot of time teaching His disciples about prayer. Please take the time to ask the Lord to lay on your heart a hunger for prayer and that He will show you the importance of prayer.

Chapter Twelve: Discipline "Plus"

There is an issue with which everyone who works with these special young people has to deal: discipline. Discipline is a difficult subject and there is an invisible line drawn in the sand which one cannot cross. Many of the youth have been reared in an environment with little structure and discipline at home. With this background at home, there is a vast contrast in ministry. In this chapter, we are going to try to scratch the surface of the issue of discipline.

One must realize that in working with "special," but not "perfect" youth, there is going to be days of progress and then, there are going to be days when nothing goes right. This ministry takes time: three steps forward and two steps back. We need to be patient as Christ has been patient with us.

Respect is very big in the inner-cities. Respect should also be very important to us. The question is, "How should respect be gained?" Once, a co-worker of mine said that he wasn't going to respect the youth until they respected him. **CROAK!** He felt because of his position or "status," he deserved respect. He was totally wrong and he didn't have a ministry with the youth because of it. Respect isn't just given. It must be done the "old fashioned" way – *we must earn it!*

The youth will test to see what the boundaries are. They want to know how you will respond to this and that. They want to know if you believe in what you say, Do you resemble the Jesus you teach them? They are always watching. These are things that are almost automatic. They are going to happen.

Let me share a classic example of how **not** to act. Too many times, people try to come in like a dictator or ruler...what they say is law and you don't question it. Sometimes, I look at it as a teacher-student relationship like back in junior and senior high school. They see it as discipline, law and order is force-fed. Now, I was fortunate to have some fantastic teachers as I grew up. We had one worker that tried this method one summer when I was in Fort Worth. Once, Eric, a five-year-old boy, got reprimanded by her and started crying with his head down. She wanted him to look at her as she lectured him. In doing this, she placed her hand under his chin to force him to look at her. At this, Eric's big brother put down his pool stick and started to approach. If it were not for another worker stepping in and consoling sobbing Eric and explaining what he did was wrong and approaching discipline mixed with love, there would have been an escalation of the situation. A couple of years later, when I was sick, I had asked another worker in the center to check on our new summer missionaries to make sure that they were doing well in Kid's Club. That night, I got a friend to drive me over to Teen Club because it was a time when the youth were able to come play basketball, pool ping-pong, hang out, and embrace the Gospel of Jesus Christ. When I got there, I found out that Miquel, a twelve-year-old boy, had "shot the bird" (the process of holding up a hand with only the middle finger sticking up) at him and he lost it. He let his anger take over and he physically picked up Miquel, threw him out the door, and told him **never** to come back. While I was there, I was blessed by the fact that Miquel came around. I was able to apologize for the behavior of my co-worker and also go to talk to Miquel about his behavior. That week, the Lord allowed me to see Miquel pray to accept Christ as Lord. Just two weeks after that, Jose, his little brother, prayed to accept Christ because he had noticed a change in his brother's life. **WHOOP!!**

We need to be careful in administering discipline. We should never let anger seep in. If we do, it can ruin the ministry.

So how are we supposed to keep order? In all situations, we need to ask ourselves, "How would Jesus respond?" Wait a minute…I know that Jesus was 100% God, but you have to realize that as Christians, we have Jesus and His power in us. Philippians 4:13 says, "I can do everything through Him (Jesus Christ) who gives me strength."[60]

---

[60] The Bible (New International Version).

I do not believe Jesus was a sissy-looking wimp that Hollywood has made Him out to be, but I do believe that He had strength and power which was under control. It takes a lot of prayer, patience, and insight. Sometimes, I think I understand a situation and respond to it, to only find out later that I did not see the bigger picture that was really happening. If one messes up in a disciplinary situation, I feel that they must go apologize to the individual and make it right. I have seen some who would not do that because of pride. If we do not handle situations in the right manner, what message are we sending?

If we try to focus on the young people as Christ sees them, I think we will be all right. When He looked at people, He looked at them in love and saw the potential within them. Just look at the men in whom He chose to invest His ministry: Peter, the impulsive; Matthew, the tax collector; and Simon the Zealot, to name a few. Once, when He was walking through a town, He looked up in a tree and saw the most despised man of the community, Zacchaeus. Zacchaeus was a tax collector, a cheat...and everyone knew it. When Jesus looked up and saw Zacchaeus, He called him by name and invited Himself for dinner.[61] Not only did this shock the townspeople – it probably gave Zacchaeus a jolt, too. When Zacchaeus encountered Jesus Christ, his life was changed. You see, Jesus loves the sinner, but hates the sin. We should also love the sinner, but hate the sin.

One thing essential to understand about when they get in trouble is that it is not because of who they are, but because of what they have done. I try to sit the person down and tell them that I forgive them and that they are special, but then at the same time, let them know that they must pay the

---

[61] Luke 19:1-9.

consequences for their actions. Once in San Antonio, I looked out the window and saw five kids using my car as a trampoline. I walked outside and calmly asked them to come in. Then, with a leader of the community, I spoke to them about their actions. I was able to show them forgiveness, but I still took each one to their home to let their parents know what happened. Even though I forgave them, they had to be responsible for their actions. God is just and full of mercy. He is our example.

When I was attending East Texas Baptist University, I went on a spring break mission trip with the Baptist Student Ministry. We went to the west side of Houston to do Backyard Bible Clubs in some government housing projects. While we were there, one older boy seemed to be a trouble-maker. Actually, he just wanted attention and that was the best way he knew of to get it. One of my friends, Tanya, caught him when he was acting better than the others and said, "I wish y'all could be as good as…" All of a sudden, his shoulders went back and he sat up straight. He looked like a struttin' peacock. From that moment on, he took pride in being good and set an example for the class. It was fantastic!

Another thing that is important in discipline is to try to see their intent, motive, what is really in their hearts. I have always tried to see what their motives are before I determine how I am going to react to the situation. So many times, it is easy to get caught up in legalism while disciplining. We just look at the wrong and fire away with the punishment. Sometimes, there are circumstances behind the wrong. For instance, while playing basketball, is seems that certain "colorful metaphors" are sounded. One thing I have to remember is that this is a normal way of life for them and that this is a part of their culture. I can't expect them to switch into Opie Taylor of *The Andy Griffith Show* overnight. It takes time for them to get adjusted to a new way of speaking. When it is just something that seems to slip out, I will ask them not to cuss, but when it deliberately comes out of their heart, a stiffer punishment is required. Usually, after a couple of warnings, I will send them home, explaining to them just why they were being asked to leave. It is hard at times, but the more you get to know the kids and what is going around, the easier it is to have discernment.

Another aspect if consistency. If you are not consistent in your discipline, then they will use it against you. It will look like you are showing favoritism to one over another. Even if you are consistent in the way you determine the extent of punishment, they will notice. After a while, they will even know what to expect from you and will make them more secure about being around you.

Always make sure that you are prayed up. We need to seek His guidance and His wisdom on how to handle ourselves each day. We need to realize that they will only be with us just a short period of the week. Many of them will be facing negative influences the rest of the week and many times, you will have to handle the overflow when they are with you. It is tough at times, but very rewarding. Always remember that He is faithful and will always be there, so fall back in His arms and rest in His rest and strength.

Discipline is a vital issue you will have to deal with as you work with these special people. Always remember to surround the discipline with love. Let Christ love through you. They will be able to tell if you really care. Many times, I've seen a youth sent home (some cussing me out while leaving,) but the next time the doors were open, they were there, too. There is a need being met that they can't get from the street – and the answer is Jesus Christ! Ask the Lord to show you His discipline and that He will give you wisdom on how to deal with these *special people*.

Chapter Thirteen: Love

BEYOND

The Judge, at last, had spoken.
The judgment was past down.
It led us to believe our King
would never wear His crown.
The throne would not behold
His power would not been gold
And He…Our supreme dignity
looked beaten – whipped and old.
But wait! Beyond the reach of mortal man
His power was set free,
And even though our King of kings,
was hanging on the tree,
Love reached beyond that dark day
beyond what eyes could see,
Beyond the cross, beyond the truth,
and saved a very bad person like me.

Billy Joe Perales

In the last chapter, we talked about how our discipline should be done in love. Well, in this chapter, we will talk about just what we mean when we say, "love." Here in America, we use the word, "love," for just about everything. We refer to "love" when we talk about pizza, movies, songs, and many other different things. I feel that it has lost its meaning. Love is very important in ministering in the inner-cities. Many people have misunderstood what love is all about. It needs to be shown and demonstrated over a period of time, so they can see the difference and let the Lord bring them to Himself.

In the New Testament, there are four Greek words which we translate as "love." The first one is "phileo." It is brotherly love, a love of friendship. It is the root word in the name of the town of Philadelphia, Pennsylvania, the city of brotherly love. Remember from 5th grade history? The next one is "eros" and this is physical love. Now, the word is a lot more beautiful word than we usually make it out to be. We have allowed the world to shape this word with its definition. The third word that is translated as love is "storga." This is a family love such as a mother or father has for their son or daughter. This, too, is a very deep kind of love. The last type of love is "agape." It is the love of the will, love of commitment.[62] It is where one chooses to love another, just like God chose to love us. He did not have to love us unconditionally. No one put a gun to His head. He chose to love us and demonstrated that love in this, that while we were still sinners, Christ died on the cross![63] Even though the *correct* meanings of these types of love should be taught like God meant for them to be, we are going to concentrate on the last type of love – "agape."

This is the same type of love that was shown on the cross – a sacrificial commitment. The love that took Christ to the cross is the same love that Christ commands that we should give to others: "My command to you is this: Love each other as I have loved you."[64] When one looks at this statement more deeply, the reality of it becomes astounding. Are we

---

[62] Interview with James Simmons, August 4, 1997.
[63] Romans 5:8
[64] John 15:12

willing to give all of ourselves to others, even though they reject us and spit in our face, even to the point of death? That is deep.

The love that Christ showed us was unconditional. He loved and died for Hitler as much as He loved and died for us. So our love should be unconditional, too. It is easy to love those whom you like, that are hungry for His Word, and growing, but also it includes the ones who cause trouble and would cuss you out in a heartbeat. I have found that consistent love can change the biggest trouble-makers. No matter what they do...we need to love them. I admit, it is tough at times. Then again, I have to remind myself that it wasn't easy for Christ either as He went through trials, beatings, insults, and crucifixion. *If they are good enough for Jesus...they better be good enough for me.*

All too often, inner-city children and youth are told by the establishment that they are no good and that they will never be worth anything. I learned a long time ago that negative statements are very powerful. It takes about forty positive statements to undo one negative one.[65] We need to encourage and build them up as much as we can. Give them an opportunity to see themselves as God sees them. Here are some examples: "Well done." "Way to go." "Great job." "Great discovery." "You are responsible." "You made the right choice." "You tried hard." "You're a good friend." "You're important to me." "I'm proud of you." "You have a terrific sense of humor." "You have a marvelous imagination." "I love you." And many, many more.

Now, don't get me wrong. It's more than just saying, "I love you," and "You're special." If actions do not show it,

---

[65] Interview with Randy Johnson, July, 1984.

then words mean nothing. We need to show them that they are special. The number one way we show them they are special is by spending time with them. If they like to play sports, then play sports with them. Find out what their interests are. If some are involved in Little League, school ball, or a program at school, it really lifts their spirits to see you come out to watch. It *shows* them that they are important. As I stated before, when you show them that you are interested in what they are interested in, it opens a door for a relationship. And once you have built a relationship, then you have a platform to share Christ.

In the previous chapter, we talked about discipline. This is a major area in which unconditional love should be shown. Too often, discipline can be done or received in anger. We need to discipline in love. They need to know that we discipline them because we truly care for them, not because we do not like them. In working with the kids, I would let the child know that they were special, that I forgave them, but they still had to face the penalty because what they did was wrong. We would encourage positive behavior while being consistent in the love/discipline.

Be aware of family events such as birthdays, graduations, and yes, even funerals. This shows not only the family, but also the community a genuine care. Now, these are not acts of passage, because they can tell in the first several minutes if you are genuine. One of my most honored moments was when I was invited to a "quinceanera." This is a celebration of the 15th birthday of a Latino girl. It is a right of passage from being a girl and moving on to womanhood. It was a great time of fellowship. Not only did it mean a lot to me to be invited, but it also meant a lot to the family and friends that I care enough to be present.

Be careful about promising things. It is devastating when we do not follow through. Much of the time, we do not even realize what we have done. I have had to really watch the way I phrase things, so I do not "promise" something about a possible upcoming even or something to get the youth excited. They remember when someone does not fulfill a promise. Let us be careful that we do not promise things that can't be delivered soon or ever.

Kids and teens can see right through people and they can tell if they are being conned. It might take time, but they will figure it out. I have been blessed three-fold because I chose to love these precious people unconditionally. When I think back over all my experiences in His ministry, I cannot really remember all the love that I showed, but I can remember ALL the love that I received.

There are a lot of lives out there with an absence of love. We need to be examples of what true love is all about. Let Jesus Christ love others through you. You might be the only Jesus that they will ever see…and you will be blessed.

Chapter Fourteen: If They're Good Enough For Jesus…They Better Be Good Enough For Me

The Lord has taken me many places and shown me many things. He has shown me His constant love and discipline. This shows me that He loves me and that I am special. The same goes for you. Now, it also goes for every gang member, every troubled teen, every person that's homeless or in government housing, in juvenile hall or death row, star athlete or cheerleader, loner or nerd. The Lord loved us ALL so much that he paid the ULTIMATE price to be with us. If people are so special to Christ, then people should be so special to us. The way we treat others is the way others will see Jesus.

Let me share a story that I heard Billy Beacham share at a Youth Camp:

One day, Jesus called Mary on the phone and she was so excited to receive the call. But she got even more excited to find out that He was coming over to visit the next day at three o'clock. "Wow! Jesus is coming to visit me!" she thought. Immediately, she started to clean the house. Dust particles were not safe on this day. The next morning, she went to the beauty parlor and had her hair done. She had no time to waste! When she got home, she put on her finest dress and jewelry. She was ready! At three o'clock, the doorbell rang and she quickly went down the stairs. But she did stop by a mirror on the way just to make sure everything was in place. As she arrived to door, she reached for the door knob, pulled the door open and there standing before her was the ugliest, most hideous, smelliest person that she had ever seen. "Oh, no, you can't be here!" she said in horror as she started to shut the door. The old man cried out, "Mary, Mary, it's me, it's me. I told you that I was coming. Don't you recognize me?" as he tried to keep the door from shutting. "No, no, you are not supposed to be here...I'm expecting Jesus," she cried.